EMPTY
TEMPLE

EMPTY TEMPLE

The Neglected Holy Spirit

Bishop Kirby Clements Sr.

CLEMENTS
MINISTRIES

Decatur, GA

Empty Temple: The Neglected Holy Spirit
Copyright 2018
Dr. Kirby Clements Sr.

Address inquiries to the publisher:

Clements Family Ministry
2000 Cathedral Place
Decatur, Georgia 30034 USA

Learn more about the authors and their ministry at
www.clementsministries.org

ISBN: 978-0-9968702-6-9

Printed in the United States of America

Contents

CHAPTER 1
Expansion of Christian Influence 1

CHAPTER 2
Historical Perspective 9
Record of Acts and the Epistles 12
The Challenge of Time 15

CHAPTER 3
Times of Revivals 19
Post Revival Responses 22

CHAPTER 4
Contemporary Observations 25
Theological Arguments 26
Function of the Spirit 30
Need for Education and Training 36
Lingering Questions 40

End Notes 43
Other Books By Clements Family Ministries 45

CHAPTER 1

Expansion of Christian Influence

The last century began with the Pentecostal Movement and an emphasis upon the baptism and ministration of the Holy Spirit, triggering a tremendous revival. Beginning with the Pentecostal Movement, there followed a series of other movements that have restored principles, as well as practices, previously neglected or abandoned by the Church that reflected the finished work of Christ.

The Holy Spirit has reformed our thinking on such issues as the Kingdom of God, spiritual authority, prophecy, evangelism, prayer, healing, deliverance, faith, miracles, covenant, worship, five-fold ministry, body ministry, unity, reconciliation of race and gender, and many other topics. During the course of time, there is an increased awareness on the unity of the Body of Christ. Of particular interest is the fact that the Pentecostal/Charismatic dimension of the Church receives an abundance of visibility and credibility.

Television, radio, conferences and other media exposure have brought the person, as well as the ministry, of the Holy Spirit into the homes, marketplaces, and even the political world, where laws and legislation are formed. As the "Spirit-filled" ministries and churches become popular, multitudes join their ranks along with a host of celebrities, entertainers, politicians, professionals and wealthy entrepreneurs.

In order to manage this explosion of growth, there has been a development of ministry programs, organizational structures and beautiful buildings.

Rising costs, associated with this development, demand that pastors and leaders preach more "vision-driven messages" to enlist the commitment and financial participation of their partners and members. With such an emphasis on productivity, growth and efficiency, a subtle anti-Pentecostal/Charismatic sentiment has become noticeable in the churches.

Once, there was corporate singing of psalms, hymns, spiritual songs and making of melodies in the hearts of believers; once, there was prophetic preaching sprinkled with words of knowledge and wisdom; once, there was the manifestation of faith, miracles, signs and wonders; and, once, there was corporate obedience to spiritual directives regarding evangelism and witnessing to the world.

Gradually, such spiritual activities have declined as the demand for more acceptability, sophistication and professionalism became greater. Indeed, there is still preaching, teaching, singing, and dancing for two or three hours on a Sunday, and there are still those scheduled "special meetings" for healing, miracles and celebration. However, congregations and leaders, who were once eager participants with the Holy Spirit, are degenerating into bands of spectators watching a religious drama. The institutionalization of the church, with its mounting emphasis on structure, programs, organization and the need for more social acceptability, reduces the Holy Spirit to a doctrine, a song, a dance, or even to a "special meeting."

This analogy seems strange at first when you consider that a casual glimpse back over the past century actually reveals an increase in new ministries, churches and outreach programs.

After all, whenever Christianity becomes a living force, the doctrine of the Holy Spirit receives some primary attention. *Yet, how can there be an increase in ministry activities and a decrease in Holy Spirit dynamics?* It is because during a century of restoration and increased popularity of charismatic activities, the Holy Spirit has become synonymous with church activities and programs.

It is possible that the multitudes have been attracted to "the loaves and fishes," and so have missed the personal experience with the One who makes it all possible. In fact, the term "Spirit-filled," which once was used to certify the presence of the Baptism in the Holy Spirit, has since been cast aside in favor of other trendy expressions. To be more specific, when was the last time a message was preached on the person and ministry of the Holy Spirit?

Most church growth has been accomplished to some degree through the transfer of memberships from one ministry to another; no one proactively seeks to know from the new members "if God gave them the same gift as He gave us when we believed on the Lord Jesus Christ" (Acts 11:17).

Whenever there is a decline in personal involvement with the person and character of the Holy

Spirit, an increase in human activities serves as a camouflage. The words of the prophet may seem to be coarse, but nonetheless true, when he declares, "Forasmuch as this people draw near me with their mouth, and with their lips do honor me, but have removed their heart far from me, and their fear toward me is taught by the precept of men" (Isaiah 29:13). Whenever there is a rise in strife, contention, division, internal moral and ethical disintegration of ministries, there is a decline in the emphasis on the person and character of the Holy Spirit. Pentecost is the manifestation of power and character.

We typically measure ministries by their attendance, programs, publications, musicians, outreach activities, political and social influence, along with a host of other factors. These are wonderful demonstrations of the power of Christian influence, not the presence of the Holy Spirit.

The rising decline in the ethics and the morality of ministries, as well as individual believers, raises suspicion concerning the baptism in the Holy Spirit. Indeed, baptism in the Holy Spirit is no substitute for sound doctrine and theological concepts. You cannot be intimately involved with Him without experiencing both His fruits and power.

CHAPTER 2

Historical Perspective

The prophet Joel foretells the outpouring of the Spirit upon all flesh in the latter times (Joel 2:28-29). Luke records how an angel reveals to Zacharias that his barren wife, Elizabeth, would bear a son filled with the Holy Spirit, even from his mother's womb (Luke 1:15). Some months later, when Mary visits her kinswoman, Elizabeth, Luke records that "when Elizabeth heard the salutation of Mary, the babe leaped in her womb; and Elizabeth was filled with the Holy Spirit" (Luke 1:15).

At the birth of John, Zacharias himself "was filled with the Holy Spirit and prophesied" (Luke 1:67). The scripture asserts that the Holy Spirit enabled Zacharias, Elizabeth, John, Mary, and even Simeon and Anna, to fulfill their prophetic roles.

Thirty years later, the fulfillment of Joel's prophesy seems to be at hand. John the Baptist announces that the One is coming who "will baptize you in the Holy Spirit and fire" (Luke 3:16). It is interesting that Luke never records John making any references to the birth, life, ministry, death, nor resurrection of the Lord Jesus. Indeed, John announces that He is the "Lamb of God that takes away the sins of the world". But John is clear that, when the earthly ministry of Jesus is complete, Joel's prophecy is fulfilled.

During His ministry, the Lord Jesus reveals to the disciples that another Comforter is coming (John 14:16-18) who will guide them all into truth, and bring to their remembrance all things (John 16:13-15). He will convict the world of sin, of righteousness and of judgment (John 16:8-11). He will refute all contrary arguments, logic and wisdom. The world is surrendered currently to a foreign power and acts in a manner contrary to its original destiny. The Comforter will correct and instruct the world through the ministry of the united, redeemed community. He will testify through the ministry of the Word, as well as supernatural manifestation, that there is only one living and true God, and that Jesus Christ is Lord and King.

Luke records that the promised event, foretold by Joel and the Lord Jesus, takes place in Jerusalem. The disciples are to be empowered with the Spirit so that they may be "witnesses in Jerusalem, and in all Judea, and Samaria, and to the end of the earth" (Acts 1:8).

Jesus commissions the disciples to be witnesses of Him, and witnesses of the fulfillment of the Scriptures in him, his suffering and death, his resurrection and the proclamation of repentance an faith in His name to all nations.[1]

Record of Acts and the Epistles

The book of Acts records the beginning of the charismatic Pentecostal community; the outpouring of the Holy Spirit upon a small band of believers sparked a revival that gradually turned the world upside down. These early Christians were radically committed to Christ, and they proclaimed the news of His life, death and resurrection with great zeal. There were acts of raw courage and exciting evangelism. These believers were also preoccupied with the presence of the Holy Spirit, who revealed Himself in dramatic ways.

Miracles, signs, and wonders were magnificent demonstrations of the credibility of the gospel and the validation of those who preached it. Believers spoke in tongues and prophesied as they were filled with the Spirit (Acts 2:4; 21:9). Judgment was pronounced upon opponents of the gospel through the Spirit (Acts 13:10-11).

The Holy Spirit is among the believers; He is helping them, leading them to maturity, and showing Himself in powerful action (Acts 2:42, 46; 5:42; 1 Cor. 11:20; 14). He guides (John 16:13; James 1:5), teaches (John 14:26; 1 Cor. 2:7-13), heals (1 Cor. 12:9), delivers (2 Cor. 4:8-18), restores (2 Cor. 12:7-9), and enables the believers (John 14:16-17; Romans 8:26-27). He is seen to be involved in discipleship (John 14:25-26; 15:26-27; 16:12-15), in commission (John 20:19-23), in the diaconate (Acts 6:3-5), in evangelism (Acts 8:15-17; 8:29-39; 9:17; 10:19, 44-47), in the exposure of prejudice (Acts 10:1-48; 11:12-17), in prophetic warnings (Acts 11:28; 20:22-24), in dealing with opposition (Acts 13:9), in validation of ministry (Acts 4:333; 15:7-9; 2 Cor. 12:12), in ministerial directions (Acts 16:6-7) and in the validation of callings (Acts 20:28; 2 Cor. 13:3).

Indeed, world evangelism is a significant purpose of Pentecost. Acts 1 through 7 records the initial Jerusalem during the Judean phase. This is followed in chapters eight and nine by the record of the Samarian mission. Finally, chapters ten through twenty-eight record the details of the apostolic witness to the Gentile world. In time, Christianity in every major New Testament center knew something of the moving of the Spirit. This included Jerusalem, Caesarea, Samaria, Antioch, Ephesus, Colosse, Thessalonica, Corinth, Rome, and the communities to which the book of Hebrews is written.

Worship is alive in the Spirit in these places (1 Cor. 14:26-33; Col. 3:16). Admittedly, there are dangers and extremes from the beginning. There is a need for moderation and structure in order to unify the diverse elements. On the one hand, there is speaking in tongues and prophecy; on the other hand, there are the fixed acts and forms of liturgy (Romans 12:3-13; 1 Cor. 12). However, Paul is able to bring together the breaking of bread, reading, proclamation, confession, prayer, doxology, blessing, hymns, spiritual songs, prophecies, and speaking in tongues with interpretation, so that the freedom of the Spirit, and the restraints of liturgy, work together for the building up of the Church (1 Cor. 14).

The Challenge of Time

While the early church is fairly unified in practice and doctrine, the death of the founding apostles and disciples, the onslaught of heresies, the infiltration of false teachers, and the inclusions of different cultures threatened this unity. Consequently, efforts were made to consolidate the faith through confessions, creedal statements, catechisms, traditions, and by the elevation of the episcopacy to a place of unquestioned preeminence. Even the idea of apostolic succession emerged as a concept to validate the accuracy and continuity of doctrine and practice. The seven councils, along with the canons, represented efforts to reach a consensus in Church polity and liturgical expressions. However, with this institutionalization of the Church, there arose an anti-charismatic sentiment. Augustine further promoted the idea that the supernatural stopped with the apostolic fathers.

In the midst of all of this, the gifts of the Spirit vanished. In fact, by A.D. 260, the charismatic dimension was no longer comfortable in the highly organized, well-educated, wealthy, and socially-powerful Christian communities.[2]

It is true that, down through the years, the Holy Spirit does not always receive the respect and priority that He deserves. During the late second and third century, the Church is institutionalized with its emphasis on rules, rights, orders, and dogmas; with such an emphasis, there is a decline in the gifts of the Holy Spirit. This is most interesting, considering the fact that the primitive Church is a worldwide fellowship of the Holy Spirit taking form in various fellowships and congregations of the one Body of Jesus Christ (1 Cor. 12:12-28; Eph. 2:1-22; Col. 1:13-18).

Yet, with time, the Holy Spirit is neglected—and almost supplanted—because of the institutionalization of the Church and other substitutes.

The early creeds, out of necessity to correct heresy, focus upon the person and nature of Christ, giving very little attention to the Holy Spirit. For example, the Apostolic Creed gives very little reference to him with only the words: *I believe in the Holy Spirit.* The Nicene Creed only declares, *We believe in the Holy Spirit, [the Lord, the giver of life, who proceeds from the Father and the Son]* With the Father and the Son, he is worshipped and glorified. He is spoken through the prophets.* There is no Chalcedon statement about the identity of the Spirit.

Nevertheless, throughout the Scriptures the Holy Spirit is symbolically and abundantly represented as the Dove (Matt. 3:16; 10:16), the Oil

(Exodus 30:25-38; Lev. 21:10; Luke 4:18; Acts 10:38), the Fire (Exodus 3:2; Mal. 3:2; Matt. 3:11; Acts 2:3), the Rain (Deut. 32:2; Psalm 72:6; Jer. 5:24; Zech. 10:1), the Wind (Isaiah 11:7; Ezek. 37:9; John 3:8; Acts 2:2), the Rivers (Psalm 1:3; 46:4; John 7:38), the Dew (Gen. 27:28; Psalm 133:3; Isaiah 18:4; Hos. 14:5), the Water (Psalm 65:9; Isaiah 44:3; John 3:5; 7:37,38), and even the Clothing (Judges 6:34; Luke 24:49).

CHAPTER 3

Times of Revivals

M any times in response to or after periods of moral and spiritual decline, there surfaces a revival of charismatic activity, but it is deficient in theological and doctrinal content. Charles H. Conn, in his book "Like a Mighty Army: A History of the Church of God, 1886-1995," describes one of the early revivals:

> Enthusiasm remained high. The services were generally of an emotional nature-yet the stabilizing influence of teaching, while far from adequate, was not altogether absent. The emotion that made the worshippers weep, laugh, and shout was not some indefinable psychological delirium; it stemmed from the exaltation they received from the sense of the presence of God.[3]

The Presbyterians came under the influence of the Second Great Awakening, which began in the Cane Ridge, Kentucky, area in 1801. William Sweet, in his history of revivalism in America, records that, at the Cane Ridge camp meeting, thousands of people fall in the state of a trance, and hundreds are given to such demonstrations as "jerking, rolling, dancing, and barking."[4] A casual visitor to the Azusa Street revival would be awestruck by the frenzy of religious zeal as men and women would shout, dance, speak in tongues, fall into trances, and give interpretation to tongues in English.

Indeed, the outpouring of the Holy Spirit, and the enthusiastic emotional response of people to the presence of God, often stimulates more sensationalism than it produces sound theology. But an interesting phenomenon occurs with the passing of time. Efforts are made to develop sound theology and strategies to accompany the spiritual experiences. There is the emergence of healing evangelists and mass evangelism campaigns which take the gospel and the power of the Holy Spirit to the nations.[5] Pentecostals begin to build colleges and universities that introduce scholarship to the dynamics of the Holy Spirit.[6] Eventually, there comes a convergence of classical Pentecostal thought and reformed theology, or, as we like to say, the "historic Church" and the "present truth Church" finally meet.[7] The power dynamic of the Holy Spirit is properly mixed with sound theological and doctrinal concepts, and there emerges ministries that proclaim and demonstrate the reality of the Kingdom of God as a past, present, and future truth.[8] Churches emerge with congregations that dance, sing in the spirit, speak in tongues, interpret tongues, prophesize, cast out demons, heal the sick, raise the dead and work miracles; they can influence the communities, nations and even the world.

Post Revival Responses

Something very interesting begins to happen again: the excitement and power of Pentecost begins to wane as the Church seeks credibility and popularity. Television, radio and the media bring tremendous exposure and acceptability. The Pentecostal/Charismatic dimension of the faith gains a broader audience. As politicians, entertainers, doctors, lawyers, educators, scientists, athletes and wealthy entrepreneurs began to join the Church, the demand for acceptability and sophistication becomes even greater. At first, the slight decline in spiritual activities is not noticeable. Indeed, there is preaching or teaching for an hour; musical and dramatic presentations are prevalent, emotionalism runs high and there is still a consciousness of the Holy Spirit. However, beyond the emotional responses to His presence, there is a very subtle decline in the Spirit dynamics among the people.

Once there was corporate singing of psalms,

hymns, spiritual songs and making melodies in the heart; there was prophetic preaching sprinkled with words of knowledge and words of wisdom; there was the manifestation of faith, miracles and healings. Amidst the corporate obedience to spiritual directives, regarding giving and receiving, there gradually grows the need for more government, ministry programs, vision-driven messages and buildings that will attract and manage the masses. These modernizations put a squeeze on the "spiritual" activities. The congregations that once were eager participants with the leaders degenerate into spectators watching a religious drama. Institutionalization of the Church occurs again.

Such a repetition of occurrences indicate a distinct pattern. Whenever there is a significant emphasis on buildings, government, and programs, there is a decline in power.

However, let it be said that there is a need for structure and government in order to facilitate productive ministry. There is a need for programs and physical buildings to accommodate the congregations. We have discovered that the manifestation of spiritual gifts without some form of direction can be counterproductive. Consequently, as leaders, we have sought to merge sound theological concepts and practices with "principles of power." We have successfully emphasized evangelism, discipleship, church growth, prayer, worship, unity, government, and even reconciliation of gender, race, creed and tongue. But have these emphases become substitutes for the Spirit? Has the Holy Spirit quietly been reduced to a doctrine, a form, or simply an emotional sensation that comes in among us on Sunday morning called "The Presence?"

CHAPTER 4

Contemporary Observations

In response to the aforementioned history, I will use one of Paul's missionary journeys, one that Luke records sometime after Pentecost Paul meets certain disciples of John the Baptist at Ephesus (Acts 19:1-7). Hearing that they know only the baptism of John, which is a baptism of repentance, Paul introduces the gospel more accurately to them, presenting Jesus as the fulfillment of John's ministry (Matt. 3:11-12; Luke 3:15-17; 7:18-23; John 3:26-36; Acts 1:5).

When Paul lays his hands on them, they receive the Holy Spirit in the true Pentecostal tradition (Acts 2:4; 8:14-19; 10:44-46; 11:17; 19:4-6). Like

Jews (Acts 4:31), Samaritans (Acts 8:14-17), Romans (Acts 10:44-46), Saul, a persecuting Pharisee (Acts 9:17), an Ethiopian eunuch (Acts 8:38-39), and now the twelve disciples of John the Baptist (Acts 19:1-6), all call upon the name of the Lord Jesus, and each receive as a birthright the baptism in the Holy Spirit. Some argue that it is a reasonable conclusion from biblical evidence that tongues are the "external and indubitable proof" of their baptism in the Holy Spirit.[9] In fact, it appears that, of all the Spirit's supernatural gifts, tongues appear first in order at Pentecost. The other gifts follow subsequently (Acts 2:4; 8:14-19;10:44-46; 1 Cor. 12-14; Gal. 5).

Theological Arguments

The Baptism in the Holy Spirit is occasionally regarded as a topic peculiar to Pentecostals or Charismatics. However, biblical evidence clearly presents it as the norm of the Christian experience. Perhaps it is because the Baptism in the Holy Spirit is viewed in such a restricted manner that the person of the Holy Spirit, along with His mission, is often neglected, denied and even supplanted.

Evangelicals and fundamentalists believe Pentecostals speak too much about the Holy Spirit at the expense of Jesus. They use the reference in John 16:13, "For he (Spirit) shall not speak of himself." However, when the Spirit is come, He will speak not as a distinct and independent Spirit, but from the common agreement of the Triune Godhead. Please note that He is the author of Scripture. When we honor the Holy Spirit, we are honoring Jesus, since He is the Spirit of Jesus (Acts 16:1).

Throughout the centuries, the Spirit becomes more confined to the Church. For example, in Catholicism the Spirit is subordinated to the ritual of water baptism. Only the bishops have the authority to bestow the Spirit. Protestants, in their reactions to Catholicism, shift their interest from water-baptism to preaching and personal faith, with authority being centered on the Bible rather than in the Church. With the emphasis on faith as distinct and prior to water-baptism, faith and preaching is exalted, and the role of baptism is decreased. The Spirit is regarded as the originator of faith—and the reality of His work in apostolic days is acknowledged—but the gifts are declared to have ceased with the apostles. Hence, in Protestantism, the Spirit becomes subordinate to the Bible, and the Bible replaces the sacraments as the principal means of grace and inspiration.

While the Catholics focus upon the sacraments, and the Protestants set forth the supremacy of the Scripture, the Pentecostals react to both extremes. They shift the emphasis from the mechanical sacramentalism of the Catholics, as well as the dead intellectual orthodoxy of the Protestantism, to the experience of the Spirit. The Pentecostals have justification for their interests (Acts 2:4; 4:31; 9:31;

10:44-46; 13:52; 19:6; Romans 5:5; 8:1-16; 1 Cor.
12:7, 133; 2 Cor. 3:6; 5:5; Gal. 4:6; 5:16-18; 1
Thes. 1:5; Titus 3:6; John 3:8; 4:14; 7:38; 16:7).

James D. G. Dunn (Baptism in the Holy Spirit,
Westminster Press) claims that the Pentecostal follow the Catholic in his separation of Spirit-baptism
from the event of conversion-initiation; they make
the gift of the Spirit an experience which follows
after conversion. According to Dunn, this seems
to be contrary to New Testament, although such a
pattern is alleged in Acts 8.

However, according to Paul and Luke, the baptism in the Spirit is not something subsequent to
— and distinct from — becoming a Christian; nor
is it something which only an apostle or bishop can
hope to bring about, nor something that happens
only in apostolic days. The gift of the Holy Spirit is
not separate in any way from conversion.

Function of the Spirit

Regardless of the theological arguments, the Holy Spirit is indispensable for the power of Christian witness. In fact, Christianity without the Holy Spirit would simply be a powerless philosophy or a wonderful idea. The Holy Spirit is God in action and power (Mark 16:15-18; Luke 24:49). It is His mission to bring to pass all the fruits of Christ's victory, including His lordship over all things (John 14:26; 16:7-14). All that Christ accomplishes with His life, ministry, death, resurrection and ascension must be manifest through the Church (Eph. 1:7-10; 19-23; 2:13-22; 3:6, 10). The evidence of salvation (individual and cosmic), with its privileges and responsibilities, is experienced by the Church; but there must also be the pronouncement and demonstration of God's Kingdom by the Church to the world (Matt. 24:14; 28:18-20; Mark 16:15-18; John 17:14-18; 20). The reconciliation of the world to God, and the privileges of His wonderful grace and power, is mediated by the Holy Spirit (2 Cor. 5:18-21). He is the executive agent of the Trinity and the mediator of all divine purposes, strategies, and agendas on the earth.

In the Old Testament, the Holy Spirit originates, maintains, strengthens and guides all life (organic, intellectual, and moral) towards God's ultimate purposes (God in action on the earth). Hence, the Holy Spirit is the dispenser of "Common Grace" (Matt. 5:45; Luke 6:35).

Common Grace is that general operation of the Holy Spirit whereby He, without renewing the heart, exercises such a moral influence on man that sin is restrained and order is maintained in social life so that God's purposes are realized.[10]

The Holy Spirit is the first person of the Trinity that we experience when we are brought into covenant with God. (John 6:44; 1 Cor. 12:3). Jesus declares the necessity of being "born of water and the Spirit" (John 3:5). Spiritual regeneration is absolutely necessary for salvation.[11] This is mediated through the preaching of the gospel by the power of the Holy Spirit (Romans 1:16; 10:10-15; 1 Pet. 1:12). The preaching of the gospel, faith, repentance, baptism in the Holy Ghost, and water are the keys that unlock the door to the ultimate destiny for the repentant sinner (Matt. 16:18; Acts 2:14-41).

It is the Holy Spirit who enables the believer to relate to the Son and the Father, and to enter into the Body of Christ. As already mentioned, the Holy Spirit guides (John 16:13; James 1:5), teaches (John 14:26; 1 Cor. 2:7-13), heals (1 Cor. 12:9), delivers (2 Cor. 4:8-18), restores (2 Cor. 12:7-9), and enables the believer (John 14:16,17; Romans 8:26-27). He is seen to be involved in discipleship (John 14:25-26; 15:26-27; 16:12-15), commission (John 20:19-23), deaconate (Acts 6:3-5), evangelism (Acts 8:15-17; 8:29-39; 9:17; 10:19; 44-47), removal of prejudice (Acts 10:1-48; 11:12-17), prophetic warnings (Acts 11:28; 20:22-24), demonic opposition (Acts 13:9), validation of ministry (Acts 4:33; 15:7-9; 2 Cor. 12:12), ministerial directions (Acts 16:6-7), and validation of callings (Acts 20:28; 2 Cor. 13:3).

At the meeting of the Sanhedrin, when the missionary endeavors of Peter and Paul comes under the scrutiny of the other apostles and elders, James demonstrates the significance of the Holy Spirit in counsel with the words, "It seemed good to the Holy Ghost and to us" (Acts 15:28).

It is the Spirit that validates callings and confirms the gospel message. This is a critical factor in understanding true apostolic authority. Contrary to ancient Roman Catholicism, Protestant reformers see apostolic foundation as the gospel of Jesus Christ; his death and resurrection are the fulfillment of the law, the only basis for salvation from sin, and the granting of eternal life.[12] The mechanical succession of apostolic authority, which is based in a direct succession back to Peter, without an understanding of the witness and teaching of the first apostles is highly suspect.

In fact, such a theology of the church, which is based on some kind of historical continuity with the incarnation through the first century apostles, tends to marginalize the Pentecost experience of the Holy Spirit. It raises suspicion concerning the role of the Holy Spirit in the interpretation of Scripture, as well as in the manifestation of the Spirit in the life and mission of the church.[13]

Some will agree with Charles Hodge, in his *Systematic Theology* (Chapter One), that the Holy Spirit has no part in determining the rule of faith, but only in its application. Hence, Hodge claims the exegesis of the Scripture under the guidance of the Holy Spirit is too subjective and unreliable. However, Acts 4:33 declares that "with great power the apostles gave witness to the resurrection of the Lord Jesus". The connection between the Holy

Spirit and the "great power" that gives witness to the gospel is inseparable.

Apostolic authority or succession is inseparable from Holy Spirit power; the Holy Spirit validates the correctness of gospel.

In our efforts to be contextual, and to relate to our audiences, we often specialize in aspects of the redemptive message and neglect to preach the full counsel of God. Each revival emphasis during the last century exerted a significant influence upon the messages preached in the churches. The revival of principles and practices of faith, healing, deliverance, evangelism, worship, unity, and others did exert their influence upon the preaching itinerary. This problem is compounded during times of building projects, where concepts of covenant and personal commitments are stressed. Although the gospel lends itself to unlimited variations, there are basic contents.[14]

It is of particular interest that

when Bishop Earl Paulk began preaching and teaching things concerning the Kingdom of God, the ministry began to experience tremendous consequences.[15] There were significant manifestations of the Holy Spirit, as well as unprecedented growth and expansion of the ministry.

This should not be surprising since the whole of the preaching of Jesus Christ and the apostles was the Kingdom of God. In the preaching of the Kingdom of God, we are brought face to face with the whole of the revelation of God. Furthermore, the Kingdom of God is inseparable from the ministry of the Holy Ghost (Romans 14:17).

Need for Education and Training

Paul declares that God has not chosen many "wise according to the flesh," and "not many mighty, not many noble," but He has chosen the "foolish things of the world to put to shame the wise, and God has chosen the weak things of the world to put to shame the things which are mighty…that no flesh should glory in His presence" (1 Cor. 1:26-29). These statements should not be used to dismiss the need for education and training among the saints. The Holy Spirit works with those who discipline themselves, along with their minds. However, the Spirit is not limited to the exploits of educational endeavors, and the validation of a minister is not dependent upon a doctoral degree.

Paul also writes that the "Spirit also helps in our weaknesses (infirmities)" (Romans 8:26). This reference to "weakness", or "infirmities", is often restricted to the inability to pray effectively, or to know what to pray for.[16] There is a broader meaning here that relates to human talents, skills, and abilities. Paul declares that he came to the Corinthians in weakness, in fear, and in much trembling; his speech and his preaching were not with persuasive words of human wisdom, but in demonstration of the Spirit and in power (1 Cor. 2:3-4). Paul was a skilled craftsman, having learned words and knowledge from Gamaliel (Acts 22:3). Yet, he does not rely upon his natural abilities to reason or to speak (1 Cor. 2:13).

Instead, he prays for the right words to use in order to make known the mystery of the gospel (Eph. 6:19). Paul knows that human abilities are weaknesses and infirmities at best. (Phil. 3:3-7); he knows that human inabilities, whether they are experiential, verbal, intellectual, or physical, are compensated by the Spirit. It is the Holy Spirit that enables the minister to preach, teach, plan, set goals, and accomplish them.

Indeed, we do not know what to pray for as we ought, and we do not know how to accomplish spiritual ministry. Regardless of human ability, without the Holy Spirit, the ministry of the preacher is simply "persuasive speech of human wisdom." The Holy Spirit is the "Compensator."

The Holy Spirit regenerates us and generates faith in the Word of God. He illuminates the believer with the knowledge of God (Romans 1:21; 1 Cor. 2:14; 2 Cor. 4:4; Eph. 5:8). The Holy Spirit renews the mind, making it capable of receiving insight not available to the un-renewed mind (1 Cor. 2:14-16). Even though the intelligence of the believer is affected by the reception of the Holy Spirit, it is not informed intellectually. Dr. Ern Baxter, an outstanding teacher and theologian who understood the Pentecostal and the historic Church traditions, would often state in his lectures that believers need their spirits and their minds baptized in the Holy Spirit. Such a statement gives clear support to the fact that the presence of the Holy Spirit in the lives of the believers is no substitute for sound doctrine. The intelligence of the Spirit is to be found in the Word. Hence, there must exist a proper relationship between the Word and the Spirit (Matt. 22:29).

Lingering Questions

Is the Holy Spirit being nudged out the work of the Church today? Does it still "seem good to the Holy Spirit and us" in our decisions and choices? Is the baptism in the Holy Spirit considered the norm or is it the exception of the salvation experience? Is the Holy Spirit the validation of ministry or is it public consensus? How much priority is given to His presence in the corporate meetings of the church? Has the need for church structure, ministry productivity, and congregational growth compromised our sensitivity to the Spirit? Most importantly, has our dependency upon modern technology and the Internet compromised our sensitivity to the witness of the Holy Spirit?

I cannot answer all of these questions personally, but perhaps you can. Let us get wrapped up with Him personally. He is neither a doctrine nor a feeling, nor is He simply a presence.

He will enable us to accomplish what Christ Jesus has already finished. That's enough!

Whenever Christianity has become a living power, the doctrine of the Holy Spirit has been highly regarded. It may do us well to refocus upon His person, character and mission once again.

End Notes

1. Michael Green, Evangelism in the Early Church (Hodder and Stoughton, 1970).

2. Ronald A.N. Kydd, Charismatic Gifts in the Early Church (Hendrickson Publisher, 1984).

3. Charles H. Conn, Like A Mighty Army (Pathway Press, 1977).

4. William Sweet, Revivalism In America (Pathway Press, 1967).

5. Daniel Edwin Harrell, All Things Are Possible: The Healing and Charismatic Revival in Modern America (Indiana University Press, 1975).

6. Stanley M. Burgess and Gary B. McGee, Dictionary of Pentecostal and Charismatic Movements (Regency Reference Library, 1987).

7. Record of my personal experience as an elder at the Cathedral of the Holy Spirit under the leadership of Archbishop Earl Paulk. A splendid neo-gothic cathedral was constructed seating over 10,000 members that demonstrated a significant convergence of Pentecostal power and liturgical patterns.

8. Earl Paulk and Daniel Rhodes, A Theology for the New Millennium (Cathedral Press, 2000).

9. Howard M. Ervin, Spirit Baptism: A Biblical Investigation (Hendrickson Publisher, 1987).

10. Particular observation of Pastor Daniel Rhodes, a pastor and theologian at Cathedral of the Holy Spirit.

11. J.I. Packer, Fundamentalism and the Word of God (Eerdman's Printing Company, 1988).

12. Roy S. Anderson, The Praxis of Pentecost: Revisioning the Church's Life and Mission (InterVarsity Press, 1993).

13. Ibid.

14. Michael Green, Evangelism in the Early Church (Hodder and Stoughton, 1970).

15. Earl Paulk, The Ultimate Kingdom (Kingdom Publisher, 1984).

16. Intercession means to "hit the mark" whereas sin implies to "miss the mark."

Other Books by Clements Family Ministries

A Prevailing Spirit - a practical and insightful journey of faith and the role of traditional and alternative cures

And He Gave Them - exploring creational order and the co-equality of men and women in the home, church and market place

A Philosophy of Ministry - examines the motivation for various aspects of church ministry and programs

Spirit Friendly Church - while people-friendly programs are effective there are activities that engage the Holy Spirit

When Prophecies Fail - Exploring the source, content, intent and response of personal and end time prophecies

The Second - a look at factors that produce cooperation rather than competition in various aspects of ministry

Spiritual Intelligence - a practical guide to understanding spiritual intelligence and various factors such as knowing God and making Him known, psychic phenomena and Pentecostal power, spiritual segregation and integration and many others

Thy Kingdom Come - exploring the various concepts of the rule of God and implications upon the attitude and behavior of the believer and the church

Discernment - insightful look into discernment and the natural world of people, ideas, beliefs, and doctrines and the spiritual world of prophecies, revelations, demons and angels

Wisdom Between Pages - a book of original sayings and short statements that will provoke faith, joy, confidence and expectation

No Controversy - a short biography of the life and ministry of Sandra Clements

Navigating the Journey - an examination of the life, ministry and demise of one of the first mega churches in America

Her Name Is Mother - a practical guide to productive parenting

The Struggle and Triumph of the Believer - an examination of some of the common challenges of faith and their solutions

9 780996 870269